C. S. Lewis'

LITTLE BOOK OF
WISDOM

First published in 2018 by
Hampton Roads Publishing Company, Inc.
Charlottesville, VA 22906
Distributed by Red Wheel/Weiser, LLC
www.redwheelweiser.com

Published by arrangement with HarperCollins*Publishers* Ltd
Text © C. S. Lewis Pte Ltd

Compiled by Andrea Kirk Assaf and Kelly Anne Leahy
Cover design by e-Digital Design
Cover illustration and lion illustration credit: Shutterstock.com

ISBN: 978-1-57174-845-4

Library of Congress Cataloging-in-Publication Data available upon request

Printed in Slovenia

10 9

MIX
Paper | Supporting
responsible forestry
FSC™ C007454
FSC
www.fsc.org

This book contains FSC™ certified paper and other controlled
sources to ensure responsible forest management.

C. S. Lewis'
LITTLE BOOK OF
WISDOM

Meditations on Faith, Life, Love, and Literature

Compiled by Andrea Kirk Assaf & Kelly Anne Leahy

HAMPTON ROADS

When all the suns and nebulae have passed away, each one of you will still be alive.

The Weight of Glory

Contents

Introduction

Upon reading the words of Clive Staples Lewis, it does not take long to feel as though you are an intimate friend, as though it is just the two of you sharing a pint in The Eagle and Child, his favorite pub, or a cup of tea by the fireside in his sitting room.

When we picture him, Lewis might be wearing a cozy dressing gown and slippers, or a tweed jacket with a smoking pipe in hand. But do not let these comforting associations fool you; Lewis is the master of laying bare human folly and getting to the heart of the matter.

Although in a most approachable manner, his wit can bite, and his wisdom can expose our doubts to the light of day. His insight can be so jarring because it comes directly from his own experience; it comes from a life deeply pondered and bravely lived.

In both the world of Narnia and in his Christian apologetical works, Lewis draws us up close to the comforting fireplace with his conversational style. Just as we've warmed up, he catches us off guard by stirring up the hot coals of truth and striking our consciences with a burning clarity.

Consider this quote:

'When a willing victim who had committed
no treachery was killed in a traitor's stead, the
Table would crack and Death itself would start
working backwards ...'

Aslan's sacrifice on Edmund's behalf atop
the White Witch's stone table invokes a deep
magic that breaks the bond of death. All
this requires little explanation to the reader,
and indeed is better appreciated without an
explanation. In this brief excerpt from *The
Lion, the Witch and the Wardrobe*, Lewis successfully

employs the Moral Imagination, seamlessly weaving profound theological insight through a captivating story.

Contemplating the wisdom of Lewis pulls us into an experience not unlike that of Eustace Scrubb—that nasty little boy who is transformed into a dragon through his selfishness in *The Voyage of the Dawn Treader*. Only when he sheds great dragon tears of repentance does Aslan appear and peel away the scaly skin.

'The very first tear he made was so deep that I thought it had gone right into my heart.

And when he began pulling the skin off, it hurt worse than anything I've ever felt. The only thing that made me able to bear it was just the pleasure of feeling the stuff peel off … Then he caught hold of me—I didn't like that much for I was very tender underneath now that I'd no skin on—and threw me into the water. It smarted like anything but only for a moment. After that it became perfectly delicious and as soon as I started swimming and splashing I found that all the pain had gone from my arm. And then I saw why. I'd turned into a boy again.'

In the pages that follow, you will find, dear reader, maps to help you make the same journey as that of Eustace Scrubb—Lewis' words of wisdom on how we should live as Christians, embrace the gift of joy, transform grief, learn how to love, see reality through the imagination, enjoy friendship, find reason to hope, recognize sin, understand the nature of God, and seek Aslan's country.

So pull up a chair by the fire; it's time for a conversation with a wise friend.

'Our drinks are at our elbows ... the whole world, and something beyond the world, opens itself to our minds as we talk ... '—*The Four Loves*

Andrea Kirk Assaf and Kelly Anne Leahy
20 November, 2017
Remus, Michigan, U.S.A.

PART ONE

Living a Full Life with Christ

Every Christian is to become a little Christ. The whole purpose of becoming a Christian is simply nothing else.

Mere Christianity

We are always falling in love or quarreling, looking for jobs or fearing to lose them, getting ill and recovering, following public affairs. If we let ourselves, we shall always be waiting for some distraction or other to end before we can really get down to our work. The only people who achieve much are those who want knowledge so badly that they seek it while the conditions are still unfavorable. Favorable conditions never come.

The Weight of Glory

The terrible thing, the almost impossible thing, is to hand over your whole self—all your wishes and precautions—to Christ.

Mere Christianity

A good, but unexamined life will be high on duty and not likely to celebrate the odd paradoxes, the ironic coincidences, and the humor of being dirt …

Surprised by Joy

The more we let God take us over, the more truly ourselves we become—because He made us. He invented us. He invented all the different people that you and I were intended to be ... It is when I turn to Christ, when I give up myself to His personality, that I first begin to have a real personality of my own.

Mere Christianity

You never know how much you really believe anything until its truth or falsehood becomes a matter of life and death to you. It is easy to say you believe a rope to be strong and sound as long as you are merely using it to cord a box. But suppose you had to hang by that rope over a precipice. Wouldn't you then first discover how much you really trusted it?

A Grief Observed

Do not imagine that if you meet a really humble man he will be what most people call 'humble' nowadays: he will not be a sort of greasy, smarmy person, who is always telling you that, of course, he is nobody. Probably all you will think about him is that he seemed a cheerful, intelligent chap who took a real interest in what you said to him. If you do dislike him it will be because you feel a little envious of anyone who seems to enjoy life so easily. He will not be thinking about humility: he will not be thinking about himself at all.

Mere Christianity

For spiritual nature, like bodily nature, will be served; deny it food and it will gobble poison.

'Equality' in *Present Concerns*

Surely arrested development consists not in refusing to lose old things but in failing to add new things …

'On Three Ways of Writing for Children' in
Of Other Worlds: Essays and Stories

Make your choice, adventurous Stranger,
Strike the bell and bide the danger,
Or wonder, till it drives you mad,
What would have followed if you had.

The Magician's Nephew

Look for yourself, and you will find in the long run only hatred, loneliness, despair, rage, ruin, and decay. But look for Christ and you will find Him, and with Him everything else thrown in.

Mere Christianity

You can put this another way by saying that while in other sciences the instruments you use are things external to yourself (things like microscopes and telescopes), the instrument through which you see God is your whole self. And if a man's self is not kept clean and bright, his glimpse of God will be blurred—like the Moon seen through a dirty telescope.

Mere Christianity

Perhaps the experience had been so complete that repetition would be vulgarity—like asking to hear the same symphony twice in a day.

Perelandra

Critics who treat 'adult' as a term of approval, instead of as a merely descriptive term, cannot be adult themselves. To be concerned about being grown up, to admire the grown up because it is grown up, to blush at the suspicion of being childish; these things are the marks of childhood and adolescence. And in childhood and adolescence they are, in moderation, healthy symptoms. Young things ought to want to grow. But to carry on into middle life or even into early manhood this concern about being adult is a mark of really arrested development. When I was ten, I read fairy tales in secret and would have been ashamed if I had been found doing so. Now that I am fifty I read them openly. When I became a man I put away childish things, including the fear of childishness and the desire to be very grown up.

'On Three Ways of Writing for Children' in
Of Other Worlds: Essays and Stories

Every time you make a choice you are turning the central part of you, the part of you that chooses, into something a little different from what it was before. And taking your life as a whole, with all your innumerable choices, all your life long you are slowly turning this central thing either into a heavenly creature or into a hellish creature: either into a creature that is in harmony with God, and with other creatures, and with itself, or else into one that is in a state of war and hatred with God, and with its fellow creatures, and with itself. To be the one kind of creature is heaven: that is, it is joy and peace and knowledge and power. To be the other means madness, horror, idiocy, rage, impotence, and eternal loneliness. Each of us at each moment is progressing to the one state or the other.

Mere Christianity

If God had granted all the silly prayers I've made in my life, where should I be now?

Letters to Malcolm: Chiefly on Prayer

If you're thinking of becoming a Christian, I warn you, you're embarking on something, which will take the whole of you.

Mere Christianity

Christianity, if false, is of no importance and, if true, is of infinite importance. The one thing it cannot be is moderately important.

God in the Dock

If we are going to be destroyed by an atomic bomb, let that bomb when it comes find us doing sensible and human things—praying, working, teaching, reading, listening to music, bathing the children, playing tennis, chatting to our friends over a pint and a game of darts—not huddled together like frightened sheep and thinking about bombs. They might break our bodies (a microbe can do that) but they need not dominate our minds.

On Living in the Atomic Age

The more you obey your conscience, the more your conscience will demand of you.

Mere Christianity

Gratitude looks to the past and love to the present; fear, avarice, lust, and ambition look ahead.

The Screwtape Letters

The sun looks down on nothing half so good as a household laughing together over a meal.

The Weight of Glory

No man who bothers about originality will ever be original: whereas if you simply try to tell the truth (without caring twopence how often it has been told before) you will, nine times out of ten, become original without ever having noticed it.

Mere Christianity

It is a serious thing to live in a society of possible gods and goddesses, to remember that the dullest, most uninteresting person you talk to may one day be a creature which, if you saw it now, you would be strongly tempted to worship, or else a horror and a corruption such as you now meet, if at all, only in a nightmare. All day long we are, in some degree, helping each other to one or the other of these destinations. It is in the light of these overwhelming possibilities, it is with the awe and the circumspection proper to them, that we should conduct all of our dealings with one another, all friendships, all loves, all play, all politics. There are no ordinary people. You have never talked to a mere mortal. Nations, cultures, arts, civilizations—these are mortal, and their life is to ours as the life of a gnat. But it is immortals whom we joke with, work with, marry, snub, and exploit—immortal horrors or everlasting splendors.

The Weight of Glory

As image and apprehension are in organic unity, so, for a Christian, are human body and human soul.

God in the Dock

Indeed, if we consider the unblushing promises of reward and the staggering nature of the rewards promised in the Gospels, it would seem that Our Lord finds our desires, not too strong, but too weak. We are half-hearted creatures, fooling about with drink and sex and ambition when infinite joy is offered us, like an ignorant child who wants to go on making mud pies in a slum because he cannot imagine what is meant by the offer of a holiday at the sea. We are far too easily pleased.

The Weight of Glory

And all the time—such is the tragi-comedy of our situation—we continue to clamor for those very qualities we are rendering impossible. You can hardly open a periodical without coming across the statement that what our civilization needs is more 'drive', or dynamism, or self-sacrifice, or 'creativity'. In a sort of ghastly simplicity we remove the organ and demand the function. We make men without chests and expect of them virtue and enterprise. We laugh at honor and are shocked to find traitors in our midst. We castrate and bid the geldings be fruitful.

The Abolition of Man

The future is something which everyone reaches at the rate of sixty minutes an hour, whatever he does, whoever he is.

The Screwtape Letters

He who has God and everything else has no more than he who has God only.

The Weight of Glory

One of the ends for which sex was created was to symbolize to us the hidden things of God. One of the functions of human marriage is to express the nature of the union between Christ and the Church.

God in the Dock

It is well to have specifically holy places, and things, and days, for, without these focal points or reminders, the belief that all is holy and 'big with God' will soon dwindle into a mere sentiment. But if these holy places, things, and days cease to remind us, if they obliterate our awareness that all ground is holy and every bush (could we but perceive it) a Burning Bush, then the hallows begin to do harm. Hence both the necessity, and the perennial danger, of 'religion'.

Letters to Malcolm: Chiefly on Prayer

A man can't be always defending the truth;
there must be a time to feed on it.

Reflections on the Psalms

The Christian is in a different position from other people who are trying to be good. They hope, by being good, to please God if there is one; or—if they think there is not—at least they hope to deserve approval from good men. But the Christian thinks any good he does comes from the Christ-life inside him. He does not think God will love us because we are good, but that God will make us good because He loves us; just as the roof of a greenhouse does not attract the sun because it is bright, but becomes bright because the sun shines on it.

Mere Christianity

I had not noticed how the humblest, and at the same time most balanced and capacious, minds praised most, while the cranks, misfits, and malcontents praised least. The good critics found something to praise in many imperfect works; the bad ones continually narrowed the list of books we might be allowed to read. The healthy and unaffected man, even if luxuriously brought up and widely experienced in good cookery, could praise a very modest meal: the dyspeptic and the snob found fault with all. Except where intolerably adverse circumstances interfere, praise almost seems to be inner health made audible.

Reflections on the Psalms

PART TWO

Choosing

Joy

Joy is the serious business of heaven.

Letters to Malcolm: Chiefly on Prayer

No soul that seriously and constantly desires joy will ever miss it. Those who seek find. To those who knock it is opened.

The Great Divorce

The reader who finds these three episodes [in which Joy occurred] of no interest need read this book no further, for in a sense the central story of my life is about nothing else.

Surprised by Joy

We are mirrors whose brightness is wholly derived from the sun that shines upon us.

The Four Loves

Never, in peace or war, commit your
virtue or your happiness to the future.

The Weight of Glory

It is simply no good trying to keep any thrill:
that is the very worst thing you can do. Let
the thrill go—let it die away—go on through
that period of death into the quieter interest
and happiness that follow—and you will
find you are living in a world of new thrills
all the time. But if you decide to make thrills
your regular diet and try to prolong them
artificially, they will all get weaker and weaker,
and fewer and fewer, and you will be a bored,

disillusioned old man for the rest of your life. It is because so few people understand this that you find many middle-aged men and women maundering about their lost youth, at the very age when new horizons ought to be appearing and new doors opening all round them. It is much better fun to learn to swim than to go on endlessly (and hopelessly) trying to get back the feeling you had when you first went paddling as a small boy.

Mere Christianity

We do not want merely to see beauty … We want something else which can hardly be put into words—to be united with the beauty we see, to pass into it, to receive it into ourselves, to bathe in it, to become part of it.

Transposition and Other Addresses

Free will, though it makes evil possible, is also the only thing that makes possible any love or goodness or joy worth having.

Mere Christianity

All joy reminds. It is never a possession, always a desire for something longer ago or further away or still 'about to be'.

Surprised by Joy

Joy is not a substitute for sex; sex is very often a substitute for joy. I sometimes wonder whether all pleasures are not substitutes for joy.

Mere Christianity

All joy (as distinct from mere pleasure, still more amusement) emphasizes our pilgrim status; always reminds, beckons, awakens desire. Our best havings are wantings.

The Collected Letters of C. S. Lewis

I call it joy, which is here a technical term and must be sharply distinguished both from happiness and pleasure. Joy (in my sense) has indeed one characteristic, and one only, in common with them; the fact that anyone who has experienced it will want it again … I doubt whether anyone who has tasted it would ever, if both were in his power, exchange it for all the pleasures in the world. But then joy is never in our power and pleasure often is.

Surprised by Joy

If you want to get warm you must stand near the fire: if you want to be wet you must get into the water. If you want joy, power, peace, eternal life, you must get close to, or even into, the thing that has them. They are not a sort of prize which God could, if He chose, just hand out to anyone.

Mere Christianity

If a thing is free to be good it is also free to be bad. And free will is what has made evil possible. Why, then, did God give them free will? Because free will, though it makes Evil possible, also makes possible any love or goodness or joy worth having.

The Case for Christianity

I didn't go to religion to make me happy. I always knew a bottle of Port would do that. If you want a religion to make you feel really comfortable, I certainly don't recommend Christianity.

God in the Dock

Those who put themselves in His hands will become perfect, as He is perfect— perfect in love, wisdom, joy, beauty, health, and immortality. The change will not be completed in this life, for death is an important part of the treatment. How far the change will have gone before death in any particular Christian is uncertain.

Mere Christianity

What we would here and now call our 'happiness' is not the end God chiefly has in view: but when we are such that He can love without impediment, we shall in fact be happy.

The Problem of Pain

Either the day must come when joy prevails and all the makers of misery are no longer able to infect it, or else, for ever and ever, the makers of misery can destroy in others the happiness they reject in themselves.

The Great Divorce

The Scotch catechism says that man's chief end is 'to glorify God and enjoy Him forever.' But we shall then know that these are the same thing. Fully to enjoy is to glorify. In commanding us to glorify Him, God is inviting us to enjoy Him.

Reflections on the Psalms

Don't you remember on earth there were things too hot to touch with your finger but you could drink them alright? Shame is like that. If you will attempt it—if you will drink the cup to the bottom—you will find it very nourishing; but try to do anything else with it and it scalds.

The Great Divorce

The very nature of joy makes nonsense of our common distinction between having and wanting.

Surprised by Joy

'Milton was right.' The choice of every lost soul can be expressed in the words 'Better to reign in Hell than to serve in Heaven.' There is always something they insist on keeping even at the price of misery …

The Great Divorce

Say your prayers in a garden early, ignoring steadfastly the dew, the birds, and the flowers, and you will come away overwhelmed by its freshness and joy; go there in order to be overwhelmed and, after a certain age, nine times out of ten nothing will happen to you.

The Four Loves

Do not dare not to dare.

The Horse and His Boy

The most valuable thing the Psalms do for me is to express the same delight in God which made David dance.

Reflections on the Psalms

Lust is a poor, weak, whimpering, whispering thing compared with that richness and energy of desire which will arise when lust has been killed.

The Great Divorce

PART THREE

Transforming Grief

God whispers to us in our pleasures, speaks in our conscience, but shouts in our pains: it is his megaphone to rouse a deaf world.

The Problem of Pain

God has not been trying an experiment on my faith or love in order to find out their quality. He knew it already. It was I who didn't. In this trial He makes us occupy the dock, the witness box, and the bench all at once. He always knew that my temple was a house of cards. His only way of making me realize the fact was to knock it down.

A Grief Observed

We are, not metaphorically but in very truth, a Divine work of art, something that God is making, and therefore something with which He will not be satisfied until it has a certain character ... it is natural for us to wish that God had designed for us a less glorious and less arduous destiny; but then we are wishing not for more love but for less.

The Problem of Pain

If you look for truth, you may find comfort in the end; if you look for comfort you will not get either comfort or truth only soft soap and wishful thinking to begin, and in the end, despair.

Mere Christianity

Talk to me about the truth of religion and I'll listen gladly. Talk to me about the duty of religion and I'll listen submissively. But don't come talking to me about the consolations of religion or I shall suspect that you don't understand.

A Grief Observed

Straight tribulation is easier to bear than tribulation which advertises itself as pleasure.

Surprised by Joy

No great wisdom can be reached without sacrifice.

The Magician's Nephew

Divine punishments are also mercies.

Surprised by Joy

We were promised sufferings. They were part of the program. We were even told, 'Blessed are they that mourn', and I accept it. I've got nothing that I hadn't bargained for. Of course it is different when the thing happens to oneself, not to others, and in reality, not imagination.

A Grief Observed

God allows us to experience the low points of life in order to teach us lessons that we could learn in no other way.

The Problem of Pain

For in grief nothing 'stays put'. One keeps on emerging from a phase, but it always recurs. Round and round. Everything repeats. Am I going in circles, or dare I hope I am on a spiral? But if a spiral, am I going up or down it? How often—will it be for always?—how often will the vast emptiness astonish me like a complete novelty and make me say, 'I never realized my loss till this moment'? The same leg is cut off time after time.

A Grief Observed

I have learned now that while those who speak about one's miseries usually hurt, those who keep silence hurt more.

The Collected Letters of C. S. Lewis

Mortals say of some temporal suffering, 'No future bliss can make up for it,' not knowing Heaven, once attained, will work backwards and turn even that agony into a glory. And of some sinful pleasure they say 'Let me have but this and I'll take the consequences': little dreaming how damnation will spread back and back into their past and contaminate the pleasure of the sin. Both processes begin even before death.

The Great Divorce

I thought I could describe a state; make a
map of sorrow. Sorrow, however, turns out
to be not a state but a process.

A Grief Observed

We're not doubting that God will do the best for us; we're wondering how painful the best will turn out to be.

The Collected Letters of C. S. Lewis

Try to exclude the possibility of suffering which the order of nature and the existence of free-wills involve, and you find that you have excluded life itself.

The Problem of Pain

Don't let your happiness depend on
something you may lose.

The Four Loves

God intends to give us what we need, not what we now think we want.

The Problem of Pain

God, who foresaw your tribulation, has specially armed you to go through it, not without pain but without stain.

The Collected Letters of C. S. Lewis

Crying is all right in its way while it lasts. But you have to stop sooner or later, and then you still have to decide what to do.

The Silver Chair

Peter did not feel very brave; indeed, he felt he was going to be sick. But that made no difference to what he had to do.

The Lion, The Witch and the Wardrobe

And yet all loneliness, angers, hatreds, envies, and itchings that (Hell) contains, if rolled into one single experience and put into the scale against the least moment of the joy that is felt by the least in Heaven, would have no weight that could be registered at all. Bad cannot succeed even in being bad as truly as good is good.

The Great Divorce

Adventures are never fun while you're having them.

The Voyage of the Dawn Treader

The sane would do no good if they made themselves mad to help madmen.

The Great Divorce

'You all know,' said the Guide, 'that security is mortals' greatest enemy.'

The Pilgrim's Regress

PART FOUR

Learning to Love

We are born helpless. As soon as we are fully conscious we discover loneliness. We need others physically, emotionally, intellectually; we need them if we are to know anything, even ourselves.

The Four Loves

Being in love is a good thing, but it is not the best thing. There are many things below it, but there are also things above it. You cannot make it the basis of a whole life. It is a noble feeling, but it is still a feeling … Knowledge can last, principles can last, habits can last; but feelings come and go … But, of course, ceasing to be 'in love' need not mean ceasing to love. Love in this second sense— love as distinct from 'being in love'—is not merely a feeling. It is a deep unity, maintained by the will and deliberately strengthened by habit; reinforced by (in Christian marriages) the grace which both partners ask, and receive, from God … 'Being in love' first moved them to promise fidelity: this quieter love enables them to keep the promise. It is on this love that the engine of marriage is run: being in love was the explosion that started it.

Mere Christianity

To love you as I should, I must worship God as Creator. When I have learned to love God better than my earthly dearest, I shall love my earthly dearest better than I do now. In so far as I learn to love my earthly dearest at the expense of God and instead of God, I shall be moving towards the state in which I shall not love my earthly dearest at all. When first things are put first, second things are not suppressed but increased.

The Collected Letters of C. S. Lewis

We may give our human loves the unconditional allegiance which we owe only to God. Then they become gods: then they become demons. Then they will destroy us, and also destroy themselves. For natural loves that are allowed to become gods do not remain loves. They are still called so, but can become in fact complicated forms of hatred.

The Four Loves

God lends us a little of His reasoning powers and that is how we think: He puts a little of His love into us and that is how we love one another. When you teach a child writing, you hold its hand while it forms the letters: that is, it forms the letters because you are forming them. We love and reason because God loves and reasons and holds our hand while we do it.

Mere Christianity

Need-love cries to God from our poverty; Gift-love longs to serve, or even to suffer for, God; Appreciative-love says: 'We give thanks to thee for thy great glory.' Need-love says of a woman, 'I cannot live without her'; Gift-love longs to give her happiness, comfort, protection—if possible, wealth; Appreciative-love gazes and holds its breath and is silent, rejoices that such a wonder should exist even if not for him, will not be wholly dejected by losing her, would rather have it so than never to have seen her at all.

The Four Loves

Do not waste time bothering whether you 'love' your neighbor; act as if you do, and you will presently come to love him.

Mere Christianity

'They would say,' he answered, 'that you do not fail in obedience through lack of love, but have lost love because you never attempted obedience.'

That Hideous Strength

I became my own only when I gave myself to Another.

The Collected Letters of C. S. Lewis

Every poet and musician and artist, but for Grace, is drawn away from love of the thing he tells, to love of the telling till, down in Deep Hell, they cannot be interested in God at all but only in what they say about Him.

The Great Divorce

Love anything, and your heart will certainly be wrung and possibly be broken. If you want to make sure of keeping it intact, you must give your heart to no one, not even to an animal. Wrap it carefully round with hobbies and little luxuries; avoid all entanglements; lock it up safe in the casket or coffin of your selfishness. But in that casket—safe, dark, motionless, airless—it will change. It will not be broken; it will become unbreakable, impenetrable, irredeemable. The alternative to tragedy, or at least to the risk of tragedy, is damnation. The only place outside of Heaven where you can be perfectly safe from all the dangers and perturbations of love is Hell.

The Four Loves

Love may forgive all infirmities and love still in spite of them: but Love cannot cease to will their removal.

The Problem of Pain

Nothing you have not given away will ever really be yours.

Mere Christianity

The heart never takes the place of the head: but it can, and should, obey it.

The Abolition of Man

Love is something more stern and splendid than mere kindness.

The Problem of Pain

To love at all is to be vulnerable.

The Four Loves

Love is not affectionate feeling, but a steady wish for the loved person's ultimate good as far as it can be obtained.

God in the Dock

The event of falling in love is of such a nature that we are right to reject as intolerable the idea that it should be transitory. In one high bound it has overleaped the massive of our selfhood; it has made appetite itself altruistic, tossed personal happiness aside as a triviality, and planted the interests of another in the center of our being. Spontaneously and without effort we have fulfilled the law (towards one person) by loving our neighbor as ourselves. It is an image, a foretaste, of what we must become to all if Love Himself rules in us without a rival. It is even (well used) a preparation for that.

The Four Loves

It is not out of compliment that lovers keep on telling one another how beautiful they are; the delight is incomplete till it is expressed.

Reflections on the Psalms

It's so much easier to pray for a bore than to go and see one.

Letters to Malcolm: Chiefly on Prayer

If God is love, He is, by definition, something more than mere kindness. And it appears, from all the records, that though he has often rebuked us and condemned us, He has never regarded us with contempt. He has paid us the intolerable compliment of loving us, in the deepest, most tragic, most inexorable sense.

The Problem of Pain

I believe that the most lawless and inordinate loves are less contrary to God's will than a self-invited and self-protective lovelessness.

The Four Loves

People get from books the idea that if you have married the right person you may expect to go on 'being in love' forever. As a result, when they find they are not, they think this proves they have made a mistake and are entitled to a change—not realizing that, when they have changed, the glamour will presently go out of the new love just as it went out of the old one. In this department of life, as in every other, thrills come at the beginning and do not last.

Mere Christianity

Those who love greatly are 'near' to God.
But of course it is 'nearness by likeness.'

The Four Loves

I know some muddle-headed Christians have talked as if Christianity thought that sex, or the body, or pleasure, were bad in themselves. But they were wrong. Christianity is almost the only one of the great religions which thoroughly approves of the body—which believes that matter is good, that God Himself once took on a human body, that some kind of body is going to be given to us even in Heaven and is going to be an essential part of our happiness, our beauty, and our energy.

Mere Christianity

Have you not seen that in our days
Of any whose story, song or art
Delights us, our sincerest praise
Means, when all's said, 'You break my heart?'

Poems

Every Christian would agree that a man's spiritual health is exactly proportional to his love for God.

The Four Loves

Christianity has glorified marriage more than any other religion: and nearly all the greatest love poetry in the world has been produced by Christians.

Mere Christianity

God, who needs nothing, loves into existence wholly superfluous creatures in order that He may love and perfect them. He creates the universe, already foreseeing … the buzzing cloud of flies about the cross, the flayed back pressed against the uneven stake, the nails driven through the mesial nerves, the repeated incipient suffocation as the body droops, the repeated torture of back and arms as it is time after time, for breath's sake, hitched up. If I may dare the biological image, God is a 'host' who deliberately creates His own parasites; causes us to be that we may exploit and 'take advantage of' Him. Herein is love. This is the diagram of Love Himself, the inventor of all loves.

The Four Loves

PART FIVE

Lessons from Reality and the Imagination

I believe in Christianity as I believe that the sun has risen—not only because I see it, but because by it I see everything else.

Is Theology Poetry?

Imagine yourself as a living house. God comes in to rebuild that house. At first, perhaps, you can understand what He is doing. He is getting the drains right and stopping the leaks in the roof and so on: you knew that those jobs needed doing and so you are not surprised. But presently he starts knocking the house about in a way that hurts abominably and does not seem to make sense. What on earth is He up to? The explanation is that He is building quite a different house from the one you thought of—throwing out a new wing here, putting on an extra floor there, running up towers, making courtyards. You thought you were going to be made into a decent little cottage: but He is building a palace. He intends to come and live in it Himself.

Mere Christianity

Reality is not neat, not obvious, not what you expect.

Mere Christianity

Remember He is the artist and you are only the picture. You can't see it. So quietly submit to be painted—i.e., keep fulfilling all the obvious duties of your station (you really know quite well enough what they are!), asking forgiveness for each failure and then leaving it alone. You are in the right way. Walk—don't keep on looking at it.

The Collected Letters of C. S. Lewis

As for all I can tell, the only difference is that what many see we call a real thing, and what only one sees we call a dream.

Till We Have Faces

The great thing, if one can, is to stop regarding all the unpleasant things as interruptions of one's 'own', or 'real' life. The truth is of course that what one calls the interruptions are precisely one's real life—the life God is sending one day by day: what one calls one's 'real life' is a phantom of one's own imagination.

The Letters of C. S. Lewis to Arthur Greeves

For the first time, there burst upon me the idea that there might be real marvels all about us, that the visible world might be only a curtain to conceal huge realms uncharted by my very simple theology. And that started in me something with which, on and off, I have had plenty of trouble since—the desire for the preternatural, simply as such, the passion for the Occult. Not everyone has this disease; those who have will know what I mean. I once tried to describe it in a novel. It is a spiritual lust; and like the lust of the body it has the fatal power of making everything else in the world seem uninteresting while it lasts. It is probably this passion, more even than the desire for power, which makes magicians.

Surprised by Joy

The greatest service we can do to education today is to teach fewer subjects. No one has time to do more than a very few things well before he is twenty, and when we force a boy to be a mediocrity in a dozen subjects, we destroy his standards, perhaps for life.

Surprised by Joy

Thirst was made for water; inquiry for truth.

The Great Divorce

For me, reason is the natural organ of truth; but imagination is the organ of meaning. Imagination, producing new metaphors or revivifying old, is not the cause of truth, but its condition.

'Bluspels and Flalansferes: A Semantic Nightmare'
in *Rehabilitations*

Enough had been thought, and said, and felt, and imagined. It was about time that something should be done.

Surprised by Joy

Courage is not simply one of the virtues but the form of every virtue at the testing point, which means at the point of highest reality.

The Screwtape Letters

I was by now too experienced in literary criticism to regard the Gospels as myths. They had not the mythical taste. And yet the very matter which they set down in their artless, historical fashion ... was precisely the matter of the great myths. If ever a myth had become fact, had been incarnated, it would be just like this.... Here and here only in all time the myth must have become fact; the Word, flesh; God, Man. This is not 'a religion,' nor 'a philosophy.' It is the summing up and actuality of them all.

Surprised by Joy

My own eyes are not enough for me. I will see through those of others. Reality even seen through the eyes of many is not enough. I will see what others have invented ... Literary experience heals the wound, without undermining the privilege of individuality ... In reading great literature

I become a thousand men and yet remain myself
… [Without this exposure to other views of
the world through literature, one may be] full
of goodness and good sense but he inhabits a
tiny world. In it, we should be suffocated. The
man who is contented to be only himself, and
therefore less a self, is in prison.

An Experiment in Criticism

There are a dozen views about everything until you know the answer. Then there's never more than one.

That Hideous Strength

Miracles are a retelling in small letters of the very same story which is written across the whole world in letters too large for some of us to see.

God in the Dock

What flows into you from myth is not truth but reality (truth is always *about* something, but reality is that *about which* truth is).

God in the Dock

Holy places are dark places. It is life and strength, not knowledge and words, that we get in them. Holy wisdom is not clear and thin like water, but thick and dark like blood.

Till We Have Faces

The heart of Christianity is a myth which is also a fact. The old myth of the Dying God, without ceasing to be myth, comes down from the heaven of legend and imagination to the earth of history. It happens—at a particular date, in a particular place, followed by definable historical consequences. We pass from a Balder or an Osiris, dying nobody

knows when or where, to a historical Person
crucified (it is all in order) under Pontius
Pilate. By becoming fact it does not cease to be
myth: that is the miracle. To be truly Christian
we must both assent to the historical fact
and also receive the myth (fact though it has
become) with the same imaginative embrace
which we accord to all myths.

God in the Dock

Such, then, was the state of my imaginative life; over against it stood the life of my intellect. The two hemispheres of my mind were in the sharpest contrast. On the one side a many-islanded sea of poetry and myth; on the other a glib and shallow 'rationalism'. Nearly all that I loved I believed to be imaginary; nearly all that I believed to be real I thought grim and meaningless.

Surprised by Joy

What you see and what you hear depends a great deal on where you are standing. It also depends on what sort of person you are.

The Magician's Nephew

The task of the modern educator is not to cut down jungles but to irrigate deserts.

The Abolition of Man

As to ... old composers like Schubert or Beethoven, I imagine that, while modern music expresses both feeling, thought, and imagination, they expressed pure feeling. And you know all day sitting at work, eating, walking, etc., you have hundreds of feelings that can't be put into words. And that is why I think that in a sense music is the highest of the arts, because it really begins where the others leave off.

Surprised by Joy

I wrote this story for you, but when I began it I had not realized that girls grow quicker than books. As a result you are already too old for fairy tales, and by the time it is printed and bound you will be older still. But some day you will be old enough to start reading fairy tales again. You can then take it down from some upper shelf, dust it, and tell me what you think of it. I shall probably be too deaf to hear, and too old to understand a word you say, but I shall still be your affectionate Godfather, C. S. Lewis.

From the dedication in
The Lion, The Witch and the Wardrobe

We seek an enlargement of our being. We want to be more than ourselves … We want to see with other eyes, to imagine with other imaginations, to feel with other hearts, as well as with our own … We demand windows.

An Experiment in Criticism

PART SIX

The Consolation of Friendship

While friendship has been by far the chief source of my happiness, acquaintance or general society has always meant little to me, and I cannot quite understand why a man should wish to know more people than he can make real friends of.

Surprised by Joy

In friendship ... we think we have chosen our peers. In reality a few years' difference in the dates of our births, a few more miles between certain houses, the choice of one university instead of another ... the accident of a topic being raised or not raised at a first meeting—any of these chances might have kept us apart. But, for a Christian, there are, strictly speaking, no chances. A secret master of ceremonies has been at work. Christ, who said to the disciples, 'Ye have not chosen me, but I have chosen you,' can truly say to every group of Christian friends, 'Ye have not chosen one another but I have chosen you for one another.' The friendship is not a reward for our discriminating and good taste in finding one another out. It is the instrument by which God reveals to each of us the beauties of others.

The Four Loves

Friendship is unnecessary, like philosophy, like art, like the universe itself (for God did not need to create). It has no survival value; rather it is one of those things which give value to survival.

The Four Loves

Friendship is born at that moment when one person says to another: 'What! You too? I thought I was the only one.'

The Problem of Pain

In a perfect Friendship … Appreciative-love is, I think, often so great and so firmly based that each member of the circle feels, in his secret heart, humbled before the rest. Sometimes he wonders what he is doing there among his betters. He is lucky beyond desert to be in such company. Especially when the whole group is together; each bringing out all that is best, wisest, or funniest in all the others. Those are the golden sessions; when four or five of us after a hard day's walk have come to our inn; when our slippers are on, our feet spread out toward the blaze and our drinks are at our elbows; when the whole world, and something beyond the world, opens itself to our minds as we talk; and no one has any claim on or any responsibility for another, but all are freemen and equals as if we had first met an hour ago, while at the same time an Affection mellowed by the years enfolds us. Life— natural life—has no better gift to give. Who could have deserved it?

The Four Loves

To this day the vision of the world which comes most naturally to me is one in which 'we two' or 'we few' (and in a sense 'we happy few') stand together against something stronger and larger.

Surprised by Joy

In each of my friends there is something that only some other friend can fully bring out. By myself I am not large enough to call the whole man into activity; I want other lights than my own to show all his facets … Hence true Friendship is the least jealous of loves. Two friends delight to be joined by a third, and three by a fourth, if only the newcomer is qualified to become a real friend. They can then say, as the blessed souls say in Dante, 'Here comes one who will augment our loves.' For in this love 'to divide is not to take away.'

The Four Loves

Next to the Blessed Sacrament itself, your neighbor is the holiest object presented to your senses.

The Weight of Glory

Friends are not primarily absorbed in each other. It is when we are doing things together that friendship springs up—painting, sailing ships, praying, philosophizing, fighting shoulder to shoulder. Friends look in the same direction.

'Equality' in *The Spectator* and in *Present Concerns*

The First [Friend] is the alter ego, the man who first reveals to you that you are not alone in the world by turning out (beyond hope) to share all your most secret delights. There is nothing to be overcome in making him your friend; he and you join like raindrops on a window. But the Second Friend is the man who disagrees with you about everything

… Of course he shares your interests;
otherwise he would not become your friend
at all. But he has approached them all at a
different angle. He has read all the right books
but has got the wrong thing out of every one
… How can he be so nearly right, and yet,
invariably, just not right?

Surprised by Joy

In a circle of true friends each man is simply what he is: stands for nothing but himself. No one cares twopence about anyone else's family, profession, class, income, race, or previous history. Of course you will get to know about most of these things in the end. But casually. They will come out bit by bit, to furnish an illustration or an analogy, to serve as pegs for an anecdote; never for their own sake. That is the kingliness of Friendship.

The Four Loves

We live, in fact, in a world starved for solitude, silence, and privacy: and therefore starved for meditation and true friendship.

The Weight of Glory

You become a man's friend without knowing or caring whether he is married or single or how he earns his living. What have all these 'unconcerning things, these matters of fact' to do with the real question, Do you see the same truth?

The Four Loves

Friendship is the greatest of worldly goods. Certainly to me it is the chief happiness of life. If I had to give a piece of advice to a young man about a place to live, I think I should say, 'sacrifice almost everything to live where you can be near your friends.'

The Letters of C. S. Lewis to Arthur Greeves

Walking and talking are two very great pleasures, but it is a mistake to combine them. Our own noise blots out the sounds and silences of the outdoor world; and talking leads almost inevitably to smoking, and then farewell to nature as far as one of our senses is concerned. The only friend to walk with is one who so exactly shares your taste for each mood of the countryside that a glance, a halt, or at most a nudge, is enough to assure us that the pleasure is shared.

Surprised by Joy

Those who are enjoying something, or suffering something, together, are companions. Those who enjoy or suffer one another, are not.

That Hideous Strength

Friendship, then, like the other natural loves, is unable to save itself. In reality, because it is spiritual and therefore faces a subtler enemy, it must, even more wholeheartedly than they, invoke the divine protection if it hopes to remain sweet. For consider how narrow its true path is. It must not become what the people call a 'mutual admiration society'; yet if it is not full of mutual admiration, of Appreciative love, it is not Friendship at all.

The Four Loves

Our merriment must be of that kind (and it is, in fact, the merriest kind) which exists between people who have, from the outset, taken each other seriously—no flippancy, no superiority, no presumption.

The Weight of Glory

Are not all lifelong friendships born at the moment when at last you meet another human being who has some inkling (but faint and uncertain even in the best) of that something which you were born desiring, and which, beneath the flux of other desires and in all the momentary silences between the louder passions, night and day, year by year, from childhood to old age, you are looking for, watching for, listening for? You have never had it. All the things that have ever deeply possessed your soul have been but hints of it—tantalizing glimpses, promises never quite fulfilled, echoes that died away just as they caught your ear. But if it should really become manifest—if there ever came an echo that did not die away but swelled into the sound itself—you would know it. Beyond all possibility of doubt, you would say, 'Here at last is the thing I was made for.'

The Problem of Pain

Friendship (as the ancients saw) can be a school of virtue; but also (as they did not see) a school of vice. It is ambivalent. It makes good men better and bad men worse.

The Four Loves

Has not one of the poets said that a noble friend is the best gift and a noble enemy the next best?

The Last Battle

It is when two such persons discover one another, when, whether with immense difficulties and semi-articulate fumblings or with what would seem to us amazing and elliptical speed, they share their vision—it is then that Friendship is born. And instantly they stand together in an immense solitude.

The Four Loves

The Order of the Divine mind, embodied in the Divine Law, is beautiful. What should a man do but try to reproduce it, so far as possible, in his daily life?

Reflections on the Psalms

Nothing so enriches an erotic love as the discovery that the Beloved can deeply, truly, and spontaneously enter into Friendship with the Friends you already had; to feel that not only are we two united by erotic love but we three or four or five are all travelers on the same quest, have all a common vision.

The Four Loves

Be sure it is not for nothing that the Landlord has knit our hearts so closely to time and place—to one friend rather than another and one shire more than all the land.

The Pilgrim's Regress

Alone among unsympathetic companions, I hold certain views and standards timidly, half ashamed to avow them and half doubtful if they can after all be right. Put me back among my Friends and in half an hour—in ten minutes—these same views and standards become once more indisputable. The opinion of this little circle, while I am in it, outweighs that of a thousand outsiders: as Friendship strengthens, it will do this even when my Friends are far away. For we all wish to be judged by our peers, by the men 'after our own heart'. Only they really know our mind and only they judge it by standards we fully acknowledge. Theirs is the praise we really covet and the blame we really dread.

The Four Loves

When you have reached your own room, be kind to those who have chosen different doors and to those who are still in the hall. If they are wrong they need your prayers all the more; and if they are your enemies, then you are under orders to pray for them. That is one of the rules common to the whole house.

Mere Christianity

Friendship exhibits a glorious 'nearness by resemblance' to Heaven itself where the very multitude of the blessed (which no man can number) increases the fruition which each has of God. For every soul, seeing Him in her own way, doubtless communicates that unique vision to all the rest. That, says an old author, is why the Seraphim in Isaiah's vision are crying, 'Holy, Holy, Holy' to one another (Isaiah VI, 3). The more we thus share the Heavenly Bread between us, the more we shall all have.

The Four Loves

PART SEVEN

Reason to Hope

When we lose one blessing, another is often most unexpectedly given in its place.

Yours, Jack: Spiritual Direction from C. S. Lewis

This is the terrible fix we are in. If the universe is not governed by an absolute goodness, then all our efforts are in the long run hopeless. But if it is, then we are making ourselves enemies to that goodness every day, and are not in the least likely to do any better tomorrow, and so our case is hopeless again … God is the only comfort, He is also the supreme terror: the thing we most need and the thing we most want to hide from.

Mere Christianity

Life at a vile boarding school is in this way
a good preparation for the Christian life,
in that it teaches one to live by hope.

Surprised by Joy

Look for the valleys, the green places, and fly through them. There will always be a way through.

The Magician's Nephew

You must ask for God's help … After each failure, ask forgiveness, pick yourself up, and try again.

Mere Christianity

It is not your business to succeed, but to do right; when you have done so, the rest lies with God.

Yours, Jack: Spiritual Direction from C.S. Lewis

Faith in Christ is the only thing to save you from despair.

The Joyful Christian

The Past is frozen and no longer flows, and the Present is all lit up with eternal rays.

The Screwtape Letters

Faith is the art of holding on to things your reason has once accepted in spite of your changing moods.

Mere Christianity

Since it is so likely that children will meet cruel enemies, let them at least have heard of brave knights and heroic courage.

On Stories: And Other Essays on Literature

Shut your mouth; open your eyes and ears. Take in what is there and give no thought to what might have been there or what is somewhere else. That can come later, if it must come at all. (And notice here how the true training for anything whatever that is good always prefigures and, if submitted to, will always help us in, the true training for the Christian life.)

Surprised by Joy

A pleasure is not full grown until it is remembered.

Out of the Silent Planet

Whatever you do, He will make good of it. But not the good He had prepared for you if you had obeyed him.

Perelandra

Who can duly adore that Love which will open the high gates to a prodigal who is brought in kicking, struggling, resentful, and darting his eyes in every direction for a chance of escape? The words '*compelle intrare*,' compel them to come in, have been so abused by wicked men that we shudder at them; but, properly understood, they plumb the depth of the Divine mercy. The hardness of God is kinder than the softness of men, and His compulsion is our liberation.

Surprised by Joy

'You have a traitor there, Aslan,' said the Witch. Of course everyone present knew that she meant Edmund. But Edmund had got past thinking about himself after all he'd been through and after the talk he'd had that morning. He just went on looking at Aslan. It didn't seem to matter what the Witch said.

The Lion, the Witch and the Wardrobe

Now we cannot ... discover our failure to keep God's law except by trying our very hardest (and then failing). Unless we really try, whatever we say there will always be at the back of our minds the idea that if we try harder next time we shall succeed in being completely good. Thus, in one sense, the road back to God is a road of moral effort, of trying harder and harder. But in another sense it is not trying that is ever going to bring us home. All this trying leads up to the vital moment at which you turn to God and say, 'You must do this. I can't.'

Mere Christianity

No good work is done anywhere without aid from the Father of Lights.

Reflections on the Psalms

Atheism turns out to be too simple. If the whole universe has no meaning, we should never have found out that it has no meaning.

Mere Christianity

There is a dignity and poignancy in the bare fact that a thing exists.

The Weight of Glory

Progress means getting nearer to the place you want to be. And if you have taken a wrong turning, then to go forward does not get you any nearer. If you are on the wrong road, progress means doing an about-turn and walking back to the right road; and in that case the man who turns back soonest is the most progressive man.

Mere Christianity

But only the strange power
Of unsought Beauty in some casual hour
Can build a bridge of light or sound or form
To lead you out of all this strife and storm …
One moment was enough,
We know we are not made of mortal stuff.
And we can bear all trials that come after,
The hate of men and the fool's loud bestial laughter
And nature's rule and cruelties unclean,
For we have seen the Glory—we have seen.

Spirits in Bondage

The Supernatural is not remote and abstruse:
it is a matter of daily and hourly experience.
As intimate as breathing.

Miracles

Our real journey to God involves constantly turning our backs on [nature]; passing from the dawn-lit fields into some poky little church ... But the love of her has been a valuable and, for some people, an indispensable initiation.

The Four Loves

Nowadays it seems to be so forgotten that people think they have somewhat discredited Our Lord if they can show that some pre-Christian document … such as the Dead Sea Scrolls has 'anticipated' Him. As if we supposed Him to be a cheapjack like Nietzsche inventing a new ethics! Every good teacher, within Judaism as without, has anticipated Him. The whole religious history of the pre-Christian world, on its better side, anticipates Him. It could not be otherwise. The Light which has lightened every man from the beginning may shine more clearly but cannot change. The Origin cannot suddenly start being, in the popular sense of the word, 'original'.

Reflections on the Psalms

Redeemed humanity is still young, it has hardly come to its full strength. But already there is joy enough in the little finger of a great saint such as yonder lady to waken all the dead things of the universe into life.

The Great Divorce

'You Come of the Lord Adam and the Lady Eve,' said Aslan. 'And that is both honor enough to erect the head of the poorest beggar, and shame enough to bow the shoulders of the greatest emperor on earth. Be content.'

Prince Caspian

PART EIGHT

Recognizing Sin

No man knows how bad he is till he has tried very hard to be good.

Mere Christianity

A thing may be morally neutral and yet the desire for that thing may be dangerous.

The Weight of Glory

Badness is only spoiled goodness.

Mere Christianity

The man who cannot conceive a joyful and loyal obedience on the one hand, nor an unembarrassed and noble acceptance of that obedience on the other, the man who has never even wanted to kneel or bow, is a prosaic barbarian.

'Equality' in *Present Concerns*

The sins of the flesh are bad, but they are the least bad of all sins. All the worst pleasures are purely spiritual: the pleasure of putting other people in the wrong, of bossing and patronizing and spoiling sport, and back-biting; the pleasures of power, of hatred. For there are two things inside me, competing with the human self which I must try to become. They are the Animal self, and the Diabolical self. The Diabolical self is the worse of the two. That is why a cold, self-righteous prig who goes regularly to church may be far nearer to hell than a prostitute. But, of course, it is better to be neither.

Mere Christianity

If we cannot 'practice the presence of God', it is something to practice the absence of God, to become increasingly aware of our unawareness till we feel like man who should stand beside a great cataract and hear no noise, or like a man in a story who looks in a mirror and finds no face there, or a man in a dream who stretches his hand to visible objects and gets no sensation of touch. To know that one is dreaming is to no longer be perfectly asleep.

The Four Loves

This year, or this month, or, more likely, this very day, we have failed to practice ourselves the kind of behavior we expect from other people.

Mere Christianity

I live in the Managerial Age, in a world of 'Admin'. The greatest evil is not now done in those sordid 'dens of crime' that Dickens loved to paint. It is not done even in concentration camps and labor camps. In those we see its final result. But it is conceived and ordered (moved, seconded, carried, and minuted) in clean, carpeted, warmed, and well-lighted offices, by quiet men with white collars and cut fingernails and smooth-shaven cheeks who do not need to raise their voices. Hence, naturally enough, my symbol for Hell is something like the bureaucracy of a police state or the office of a thoroughly nasty business concern.

The Screwtape Letters

He [the devil] always sends errors into the world in pairs—pairs of opposites. And he always encourages us to spend a lot of time thinking which is the worse. You see why, of course? He relies on your extra dislike of the one error to draw you gradually into the opposite one. But do not let us be fooled. We have to keep our eyes on the goal and go straight through between both errors. We have no other concern than that with either of them.

Mere Christianity

The safest road to Hell is the gradual one—the gentle slope, soft underfoot, without sudden turnings, without milestones, without signposts.

The Screwtape Letters

It is the magician's bargain: give up our soul, get power in return. But once our souls, that is, ourselves, have been given up, the power thus conferred will not belong to us. We shall in fact be the slaves and puppets of that to which we have given our souls.

The Abolition of Man

There are two equal and opposite errors into which our race can fall about the devils. One is to disbelieve in their existence. The other is to believe, and to feel an excessive and unhealthy interest in them. They themselves are equally pleased by both errors and hail a materialist or a magician with the same delight.

The Screwtape Letters

It is ... the practical and prudential cares of this world, and even the smallest and most prosaic of those cares, that are the great distraction. The gnat-like cloud of petty anxieties and decisions about the conduct of the next hour have interfered with my prayers more often than any passion or appetite whatever.

The Four Loves

When you are arguing against God you are arguing against the very power that makes you able to argue at all.

Mere Christianity

To be a Christian means to forgive the inexcusable, because God has forgiven the inexcusable in you.

Essays on Forgiveness

Mankind is so fallen that no man can be trusted with unchecked power over his fellows. Aristotle said that some people were only fit to be slaves. I do not contradict him. But I reject slavery because I see no men fit to be masters.

'Equality' in *The Spectator*

Pride gets no pleasure out of having something, only out of having more of it than the next man.

Mere Christianity

If God forgives us we must forgive ourselves. Otherwise it's like setting up ourselves as a higher tribunal than Him.

The Collected Letters of C. S. Lewis

All mortals tend to turn into the thing they are pretending to be.

The Screwtape Letters

To walk out of His will is to walk into nowhere.

Perelandra

Everyone says forgiveness is a lovely idea, until they have something to forgive.

Mere Christianity

In the long run the answer to all those who object to the doctrine of hell, is itself a question: What are you asking God to do? To wipe out their past sins and, at all costs, to give them a fresh start, smoothing every difficulty and offering every miraculous help? But He has done so, on Calvary. To forgive them? They will not be forgiven. To leave them alone? Alas, I am afraid that is what He does.

The Problem of Pain

If the Divine call does not make us better, it will make us very much worse. Of all bad men, religious bad men are the worst. Of all created beings, the wickedest is one who originally stood in the immediate presence of God.

Reflections on the Psalms

In our own case we accept excuses too easily; in other people's, we do not accept them easily enough.

The Weight of Glory

It is safe to tell the pure in heart that they shall see God, for only the pure in heart want to.

The Problem of Pain

If a man thinks he is not conceited, he is very conceited indeed.

Mere Christianity

Jesus Christ did not say, 'Go into all the world and tell the world that it is quite right.'

God in the Dock

Each day we are becoming a creature of splendid glory or one of unthinkable horror.

Mere Christianity

We laugh at honor and are shocked to find traitors in our midst.

The Abolition of Man

When we Christians behave badly, or fail to behave well, we are making Christianity unbelievable to the outside world.

Mere Christianity

There is but one good; that is God. Everything else is good when it looks to Him and bad when it turns from Him.

The Great Divorce

I remember Christian teachers telling me long ago that I must hate a bad man's actions but not hate the bad man: or, as they would say, hate the sin but not the sinner ... I used to think this a silly, straw-splitting distinction: how could you hate what a man did and not hate the man? But years later it occurred to me that there was one man to whom I had been doing this all my life—

namely myself. However much I might dislike my own cowardice or conceit or greed, I went on loving myself. There had never been the slightest difficulty about it. In fact the very reason why I hated the things was that I loved the man. Just because I loved myself, I was sorry to find that I was the sort of man who did those things.

Mere Christianity

I think the art of life consists in tackling each immediate evil as well as we can.

The Weight of Glory

We have a strange illusion that mere time cancels sin. But mere time does nothing either to the fact or to the guilt of a sin.

The Problem of Pain

PART NINE

Finding God

Y ou may forget that you are at every
moment totally dependent on God.

Mere Christianity

I am trying here to prevent anyone saying the really foolish thing that people often say about Him: 'I'm ready to accept Jesus as a great moral teacher, but I don't accept His claim to be God.' That is the one thing we must not say. A man who was merely a man and said the sort of things Jesus said would not be a great moral teacher. He would be either a lunatic—on a level with the man who says he is a poached egg—or else he would be the Devil of Hell. You must make your choice. Either this man was, and is, the Son of God: or else a madman or something worse. You can shut Him up for a fool, you can spit at Him and kill Him as a demon; or you can fall at His feet and call Him Lord and God. But let us not come with any patronizing nonsense about His being a great human teacher. He has not left that open to us. He did not intend to.

Mere Christianity

Relying on God has to begin all over again every day as if nothing had yet been done.

The Collected Letters of C. S. Lewis

I was driven to Whipsnade one sunny morning. When we set out I did not believe that Jesus Christ is the son of God, and when we reached the zoo I did. Yet I had not exactly spent the journey in thought. Nor in great emotion. 'Emotional' is perhaps the last word we can apply to some of the most important events. It was more like when a man, after a long sleep, still lying motionless in bed, becomes aware that he is now awake.

Surprised by Joy

A proud man is always looking down on things and people: and, of course, as long as you are looking down, you cannot see something that is above you.

Mere Christianity

What do people mean when they say, 'I am not afraid of God because I know He is good'? Have they never even been to a dentist?

A Grief Observed

I had approached God, or my idea of God, without love, without awe, even without fear. He was, in my mental picture of this miracle, to appear neither as Savior nor as Judge, but merely as a magician; and when He had done what was required of Him I supposed He would simply—well, go away. It never crossed my mind that the tremendous contact which I solicited should have any consequences beyond restoring the status quo.

Surprised by Joy

The Christian is in a different position from other people who are trying to be good. They hope, by being good, to please God if there is one; or—if they think there is not—at least they hope to deserve approval from good men. But the Christian thinks any good he does comes from the Christ-life inside him. He does not think God will love us because we are good, but that God will make us good because He loves us; just as the roof of a greenhouse does not attract the sun because it is bright, but becomes bright because the sun shines on it.

Mere Christianity

I do not think the resemblance between the Christian and the merely imaginative experience is accidental. I think that all things, in their own way, reflect heavenly truth, the imagination not least. 'Reflect' is the important word. This lower life of the imagination is not a beginning of, nor a step toward, the higher life of the spirit, merely an image.

Surprised by Joy

Human history is the long terrible story of man trying to find something other than God which will make him happy.

Mere Christianity

We have two bits of evidence about the Somebody. One is the universe He has made. If we used that as our only clue, I think we should have to conclude that He was a great artist (for the universe is a very beautiful place), but also that He is quite merciless and no friend to man (for the universe is a very dangerous and terrifying place.) ... The other bit of evidence is that Moral Law which He has put in our minds. And this is a better bit of evidence than the other, because it is inside information. You find out more about God from the Moral Law than from the universe in general just as you find out more about a man by listening to his conversation than by looking at a house he has built.

Mere Christianity

I know now, Lord, why you utter no answer. You are yourself the answer. Before your face questions die away. What other answers would suffice? Only words, words; to be led out to battle against other words.

Till We Have Faces

There have been men before ... who got so interested in proving the existence of God that they came to care nothing for God himself ... as if the good Lord had nothing to do but to exist. There have been some who were so preoccupied with spreading Christianity that they never gave a thought to Christ.

The Great Divorce

God made us: invented us as a man invents an engine. A car is made to run on petrol, and it would not run properly on anything else. Now God designed the human machine to run on Himself.

Mere Christianity

If He who in Himself can lack nothing chooses to need us, it is because we need to be needed.

The Problem of Pain

Christians believe that the living, dynamic activity of love has been going on in God forever and has created everything else. And that, by the way, is perhaps the most important difference between Christianity and all other religions: that in Christianity God is not an impersonal thing nor a static thing—not even just one person—but a dynamic pulsating activity, a life, a kind of drama, almost, if you will not think me irreverent, a kind of dance ... [The] pattern of this three-personal life is ... the great fountain of energy and beauty spurting up at the very center of reality.

Mere Christianity

God will look to every soul like its first love because He is its first love.

The Problem of Pain

God has infinite attention to spare for each one of us. You are as much alone with Him as if you were the only being He had ever created.

Mere Christianity

We regard God as an airman regards his parachute; it's there for emergencies, but he hopes he'll never have to use it.

The Problem of Pain

The instrument through which you see God is your whole self. And if a man's self is not kept clean and bright, his glimpse of God will be blurred.

Mere Christianity

To ask that God's love should be content with us as we are is to ask that God should cease to be God: because He is what He is, His love must, in the nature of things, be impeded and repelled, by certain stains in our present character, and because He already loves us He must labor to make us lovable … What we would here and now call our 'happiness' is not the end God chiefly has in view: but when we are such as He can love without impediment, we shall in fact be happy.

The Problem of Pain

God cannot give us a happiness and peace apart from Himself, because it is not there. There is no such thing.

Mere Christianity

We may ignore, but we can nowhere evade, the presence of God. The world is crowded with Him. He walks everywhere incognito.

Letters to Malcolm: Chiefly on Prayer

It cost God nothing, so far as we know, to create nice things: but to convert rebellious wills cost Him crucifixion.

Mere Christianity

What seem our worst prayers may really be, in God's eyes, our best. Those, I mean, which are least supported by devotional feeling. For these may come from a deeper level than feeling. God sometimes seems to speak to us most intimately when He catches us, as it were, off our guard.

Letters to Malcolm: Chiefly on Prayer

When Christ died, He died for you individually just as much as if you had been the only person in the world.

Mere Christianity

It is when we notice the dirt that God is most present in us; it is the very sign of His presence.

The Collected Letters of C. S. Lewis

Though our feelings come and go, His love for us does not.

Mere Christianity

A man can no more diminish God's glory by refusing to worship Him than a lunatic can put out the sun by scribbling the word 'darkness' on the walls of his cell.

The Problem of Pain

If you take nature as a teacher she will teach you exactly the lessons you had already decided to learn; this is only another way of saying that nature does not teach. The tendency to take her as a teacher is obviously very easily grafted on to the experience we call 'love of nature'. But it is only a graft. While we are actually subjected to them, the 'moods' and 'spirits' of nature point no morals. Overwhelming gaiety, insupportable grandeur, sombre desolation are flung at you. Make what you can of them, if you must make at all. The only imperative that nature utters is, 'Look. Listen. Attend.' … A true philosophy may sometimes validate an experience of nature; an experience of nature cannot validate a philosophy.

The Four Loves

To say that God has created her is not to say that she is unreal, but precisely that she is real. Would you make God less creative than Shakespeare or Dickens? What He creates is created in the round: it is far more concrete than Falstaff or Sam Weller ... God's creative freedom is to be conceived as the freedom of a poet: the freedom to create a consistent, positive thing with its own inimitable flavor ... It would be a miserable error to suppose that the dimensions of space and time, the death and rebirth of vegetation, the unity

in multiplicity of organisms, the union in
opposition of sexes, and the color of each
particular apple in Herefordshire this autumn,
were merely a collection of useful devices
forcibly welded together. They are the very
idiom, almost the facial expression, the smell
or taste, of an individual thing. The quality
of Nature is present in them all just as the
Latinity of Latin is present in every inflection
or the 'Correggiosity' of Correggio in every
stroke of the brush.

Miracles

Death and resurrection are what the story is about and had we but eyes to see it, this has been hinted on every page, met us, in some disguise, at every turn, and even been muttered in conversations between such minor characters (if they are minor characters) as the vegetables.

Miracles

There is no good trying to be more spiritual than God. God never meant man to be a purely spiritual creature. That is why He uses material things like bread and wine to put the new life into us. We may think this rather crude and unspiritual. God does not: He invented eating. He likes matter. He invented it.

Mere Christianity

No thing or event is first or highest in a sense which forbids it to be also last and lowest. The partner who bows to Man in one movement of the dance receives Man's reverences in another. To be high or central means to abdicate continually: to be low means to be raised: all good masters are servants: God washes the feet of men.

Miracles

What does not satisfy when we find it,
was not the thing we were desiring.

The Pilgrim's Regress

An impersonal God—well and good. A subjective God of beauty, truth, and goodness, inside our own heads—better still. A formless life-force surging through us, a vast power which we can tap—best of all. But God himself, alive, pulling at the other end of the cord, perhaps approaching at an infinite speed, the hunter, King, husband—that is quite another matter.

Miracles

The Life-Force is a sort of tame God. You can switch it on when you want, but it will not bother you. All the thrills of religion and none of the cost. Is the Life-Force the greatest achievement of wishful thinking the world has yet seen?

Mere Christianity

It is hardly complimentary to God that we should choose him as an alternative to hell. Yet even this he accepts. The creature's illusion of self-sufficiency must, for the creature's sake, be shattered. And by trouble, or fear of trouble on earth, by crude fear of the eternal flames, God shatters it, unmindful of his glory's diminution. I call this "divine humility", because it's a poor thing to strike our colours to God when the ship is going down under us, a poor thing to come to him as a last resort, to offer up our own when it is no longer worth keeping. If God were proud, he would hardly have us on such terms. But he is not proud. He stoops to conquer. He would have us even though we have shown that we prefer everything else to him, and come to him because there is nothing better now to be had.

The Problem of Pain

PART TEN

Aslan's Country

Onward Toward Heaven

The sweetest thing in all my life has been the longing—to reach the Mountain, to find the place where all the beauty came from—my country, the place where I ought to have been born. Do you think it all meant nothing, all the longing? The longing for home? For indeed it now feels not like going, but like going back.

Till We Have Faces

At present we are on the outside of the world, the wrong side of the door. We discern the freshness and purity of morning, but they do not make us fresh and pure. We cannot mingle with the splendors we see. But all the leaves of the New Testament are rustling with the rumor that it will not always be so. Someday, God willing, we shall get in.

The Weight of Glory

If you read history you will find that the Christians who did most for the present world were just those who thought most of the next … It is since Christians have largely ceased to think of the other world that they have become so ineffective in this. Aim at Heaven and you will get earth 'thrown in': aim at earth and you will get neither.

Mere Christianity

This was the very reason why you were brought to Narnia, that by knowing me here for a little, you may know me better there.

The Voyage of the Dawn Treader

All their life in this world and all their adventures in Narnia had only been the cover and the title page: now at last they were beginning Chapter One of the Great Story which no one on earth has read: which goes on for ever: in which every chapter is better than the one before.

The Last Battle

If I find in myself desires which nothing in this world can satisfy, the only logical explanation is that I was made for another world.

Mere Christianity

All these toys were never intended to possess my heart. My true good is in another world, and my only real treasure is Christ.

The Problem of Pain

One road leads home and a thousand roads lead into the wilderness.

The Pilgrim's Regress

Looking for God—or Heaven—by exploring space is like reading or seeing all Shakespeare's plays in the hope that you will find Shakespeare as one of the characters or Stratford as one of the places. Shakespeare is in one sense present at every moment in every play.

'The Seeing Eye' in *Christian Reflections*

The choice of ways is before you. Neither is closed. Any man may choose eternal death. Those who choose it will have it. But if ye are trying to leap on into Eternity, if ye are trying to see the final state of all things as it will be (for so ye must speak) when there are no more possibilities left but only the Real, then ye ask what cannot be answered to mortal ears. Time is the very lens through which ye see—small and clear, as men see through the wrong end of a telescope—something that would otherwise be too big for ye to see at all. That thing is Freedom: the gift whereby ye most resemble your Maker and are yourselves parts of eternal reality. But ye can see it only through the lens of Time, in a little clear picture, through the inverted telescope. It is a picture of moments following one another and yourself in each moment making some choice that might have been otherwise. Neither the temporal succession nor the phantom of what ye might have chosen and didn't is itself Freedom. They are a lens. The picture is a symbol: but it's truer than any philosophical theorem (or, perhaps, than any mystic's vision) that claims to go behind it. For every attempt to see the shape of eternity except through the lens of Time destroys your knowledge of Freedom.

The Great Divorce

'But what of the poor Ghosts who never get into the omnibus at all?'
'Everyone who wishes it does. Never fear. There are only two kinds of people in the end: those who say to God, "Thy will be done," and those to whom God says, in the end, "Thy will be done. All that are in Hell, choose it. Without that self-choice there could be no Hell.'

The Great Divorce

The sense that in this universe we are treated as strangers, the longing to be acknowledged, to meet with some response, to bridge some chasm that yawns between us and reality, is part of our inconsolable secret. And surely, from this point of view, the promise of glory, in the sense described, becomes highly relevant to our deep desire. For glory meant good report with God, acceptance by God, response, acknowledgment, and welcome into the heart of things. The door on which we have been knocking all our lives will open at last.

The Weight of Glory

Some people talk as if meeting the gaze of absolute goodness would be fun. They need to think again. They are still only playing with religion. Goodness is either the great safety or the great danger—according to the way you react to it.

Mere Christianity

There have been times when I think we do not desire heaven; but more often I find myself wondering whether, in our heart of hearts, we have ever desired anything else ... It is the secret signature of each soul, the incommunicable and unappeasable want, the thing we desired before we met our wives or made our friends or chose our work, and which we shall still desire on our deathbeds, when the mind no longer knows wife or friend or work.

The Problem of Pain

'Then those people are right who say that Heaven and Hell are only states of mind?'
'Hush,' he said sternly. 'Do not blaspheme. Hell is a state of mind—ye never said a truer word. And every state of mind, left to itself, every shutting up of the creature within the dungeon of its own mind—is, in the end, Hell. But Heaven is not a state of mind. Heaven is reality itself. All that is fully real is Heavenly.'

The Great Divorce

To have Faith in Christ means, of course, trying to do all that He says. There would be no sense in saying you trusted a person if you would not take his advice. Thus if you have really handed yourself over to Him, it must follow that you are trying to obey Him. But trying in a new way, a less worried way. Not doing these things in order to be saved, but because He has begun to save you already. Not hoping to get to Heaven as a reward for your actions, but inevitably wanting to act in a certain way because a first faint gleam of Heaven is already inside you.

Mere Christianity

'Son,' he said, 'ye cannot in your present state understand eternity ... That is what mortals misunderstand. They say of some temporal suffering, 'No future bliss can make up for it,' not knowing that Heaven, once attained, will work backwards and turn even that agony into a glory. And of some sinful pleasure they say, 'Let me have but this and I'll take the consequences': little dreaming how damnation will spread back and back into their past and contaminate the pleasure of the sin. Both processes begin even before death. The good man's past begins to change so that his forgiven sins and remembered sorrows take on the quality of Heaven: the bad man's past already conforms to his badness and is filled only with dreariness. And that is why ... the Blessed will say, 'We have never lived anywhere except in Heaven, and the Lost, 'We were always in Hell.' And both will speak truly.

The Great Divorce

All your life an unattainable ecstasy has hovered just beyond the grasp of your consciousness. The day is coming when you will wake to find, beyond all hope, that you have attained it, or else, that it was within your reach and you have lost it forever.

The Problem of Pain

We know nothing of religion here: we only think of Christ.

The Great Divorce

To enter heaven is to become more human than you ever succeeded in being on earth; to enter hell, is to be banished from humanity.

The Problem of Pain

I believe, to be sure, that any man who reaches Heaven will find that what he abandoned (even in plucking out his right eye) has not been lost: that the kernel of what he was really seeking even in his most depraved wishes will be there, beyond expectation, waiting for him in 'the High Countries'.

The Great Divorce

Your place in heaven will seem to be made for you and you alone, because you were made for it—made for it stitch by stitch as a glove is made for a hand.

The Problem of Pain

But I will not tell you how long or short the way will be; only that it lies across a river. But do not fear that, for I am the great Bridge Builder.

The Voyage of the Dawn Treader

For the entrance is low: we must stoop till we are no taller than children to get in.

Reflections on the Psalms

If we insist on keeping Hell (or even earth), we shall not see Heaven: if we accept Heaven, we shall not be able to retain even the smallest and most intimate souvenirs of Hell.

The Great Divorce

And how could we endure to live and let time pass if we were always crying for one day or one year to come back—if we did not know that every day in a life fills the whole life with expectation and memory and that these are that day?

Out of the Silent Planet

In heaven the whole man is to drink joy from the Fountain of Joy.

The Weight of Glory

The Complete Works of

C. S. Lewis

The Chronicles of Narnia: The Horse and His Boy

The Chronicles of Narnia: The Magician's Nephew

The Chronicles of Narnia: The Last Battle

The Four Loves

The Great Divorce

That Hideous Strength

The Pilgrim's Regress

The Problem of Pain

The Screwtape Letters: Letters from a Senior to a Junior Devil

The Space Trilogy

The Weight of Glory

Bibliography

A Grief Observed (1961)

An Experiment in Criticism (2012)

Christian Behaviour (1943)

Christian Reflections (1967)

'Equality' in *The Spectator* (1943)

Essays on Forgiveness (1960)

God in the Dock: Essays on Theology and Ethics (1970)

Is Theology Poetry? (1944)

Letters of C. S. Lewis (2017)

Letters to an American Lady (1967)

Letters to Malcolm: Chiefly on Prayer (1964)

Mere Christianity: A Revised and Amplified Edition, with a New Introduction, of the Three Books, Broadcast Talks, Christian Behaviour and Beyond Personality (1952; based on radio talks of 1941–1944)

Miracles: A Preliminary Study (1947, revised 1960)

'On Living in the Atomic Age' in *Present Concerns* (2002)

On Stories: and Other Essays on Literature (ed. Walter Hooper, 1966)

Out of the Silent Planet (1938)

Perelandra (aka *Voyage to Venus*) (1943)

Poems (2017)

Reflections on the Psalms (1958)

Spirits in Bondage (1919)

Surprised by Joy: The Shape of My Early Life (1955; autobiography)

That Hideous Strength (1945)

The Abolition of Man (1943)

The Case for Christianity (1942)

The Collected Letters of C. S. Lewis (2005)

The Four Loves (1960)

The Great Divorce (1945)

The Horse and His Boy (1954)

The Joyful Christian (1984)

The Last Battle (1956)

The Letters of C. S. Lewis to Arthur Greeves (1979)

The Lion, the Witch and the Wardrobe (1950)

The Magician's Nephew (1955)

The Pilgrim's Regress (1933)

The Problem of Pain (1940)

The Screwtape Letters (1942)

The Voyage of the Dawn Treader (1952)

The Weight of Glory and Other Addresses (1980)

Till We Have Faces (1956)

Transposition and Other Addresses (1949)

Yours, Jack: Spiritual Direction from C. S. Lewis (2008)

About the Compilers

Andrea Kirk Assaf first fell in love with the work of C. S. Lewis when she spent a summer indoors with mononucleosis at the age of thirteen. Wandering through the world of Narnia was a wonderful compensation, and the imagery and beautiful truths found in the pages of *The Voyage of the Dawn Treader* remain fresh in her mind to this day. Andrea is a writer and editor who splits her year between a farm in Remus, Michigan, U.S.A. and the Eternal City of Rome, with her husband and their four children. She is also the author of *Pope Francis' Little Book of Wisdom*, *Pope Francis' Little Book of Compassion*, *The Saints' Little Book of Wisdom* and *Jesus' Little Book of Wisdom*.

Kelly Anne Leahy graduated from Villanova University in 2014. During her time studying in the Humanities Department, she read C. S. Lewis' works and was profoundly impacted by his ability to convey truth in a manner that is simultaneously imaginative and direct. Lewis' ideas encouraged her interest in the moral imagination in literature, leading to a fellowship studying this concept at the Russell Kirk Center for Cultural Renewal in Mecosta, Michigan, U.S.A. Kelly Anne currently resides in Philadelphia, Pennsylvania, where she works as a professional fundraiser for the Intercollegiate Studies Institute. She is the co-compiler of *The Saints' Little Book of Wisdom*.

Reader's Journal

The great thing, if one can, is to stop regarding all the unpleasant things as interruptions of one's 'own', or 'real' life. The truth is of course that what one calls the interruptions are precisely one's real life—the life God is sending one day by day …

The Letters of C. S. Lewis to Arthur Greeves

In the pages that follow, dear reader, we invite you to reflect on these words of advice and record moments of the life that God is sending you day by day.

Other titles in the
LITTLE BOOK OF WISDOM series:

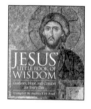

JESUS'
LITTLE BOOK
OF WISDOM
ISBN: 978-1-57174-826-3

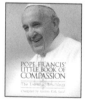

POPE FRANCIS'
LITTLE BOOK
OF COMPASSION
ISBN: 978-1-57174-778-5

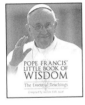

POPE FRANCIS' LITTLE BOOK OF WISDOM

ISBN: 978-1-57174-738-9

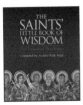

THE SAINTS' LITTLE BOOK OF WISDOM

ISBN: 978-1-57174-763-1